Doc Moves to the Mountains

Written by:
Pam Lather

Illustrated by:
Anna Welsh

This book is dedicated to the

children and animals

who are in search of

a forever home.

Doc

This book is based on the true story of "Doc", a 1600 pound Belgian draft horse who moved from the Outer Banks of the Carolina Coast to the Blue Ridge Mountains of Western North Carolina to improve his breathing.

Doc with Pam

Doc found his forever home at Southern Sun Farm Sanctuary.

Doc is a big horse with a big personality and a big heart. He is kind, gentle and very mischievous!

****

ISBN # 978-0-578-94710-5

About the Author:

Pam and her husband, Ken, retired to the Ashe County, North Carolina area from Ohio. They both volunteer at Southern Sun Farm Sanctuary.
Professionally, Pam was a court reporter for over 40 years working in the court system. She became an advocate for the plight of abused and neglected children in finding a forever home. She loves Doc and his antics as well as the mission of Southern Sun Farm Sanctuary.
Creating a children's book about them both was a new challenge, while keeping the focus on finding safe, forever homes for children and animals.

About the Illustrator:

Anna was a Pre-K, K and first grade public schoolteacher for 18 years. After teaching, she opened The Blue House Art Studio for children and adults to have a creative space to use art as an expressive outlet. She has always loved reading children's books to her students and is thrilled to be able to be a part of sharing Doc's story through his book!

My name is Doc.
I am a very big draft horse.

I lived and worked on the Outer Banks
of North Carolina by the ocean.

My friends and I gave horseback
rides on the beach.
All the boys and girls laughed in the sunshine
and we had lots of fun!

And at the
end of the
day, we
rested.

We ate hay
and apples.

I like red
apples!

But I started having trouble breathing.
It got harder and harder to do my job.

What would I do? Where would I go?

Would I find a forever home?

My beach owner called Miss Ann at
Southern Sun Farm Sanctuary.
It was in the mountains of North Carolina.
I am very big but I am very gentle.
Would she take a horse like me?

I do hope she knows I like apples!

Miss Ann said, "Of course Doc can come and live with us! We have horses, ponies, Amos the dog, cats, chickens, and a donkey. And we even have apples."

I do love apples!

I wondered what the mountains are like?

Are they beautiful like the ocean?

Would I have friends?

Is it hot or cold there?

Would I be able to breathe better?

I said goodbye to my friends and
walked into a horse trailer.
It took me across the State of
North Carolina.

It was a long, long ride to get
to the mountains.

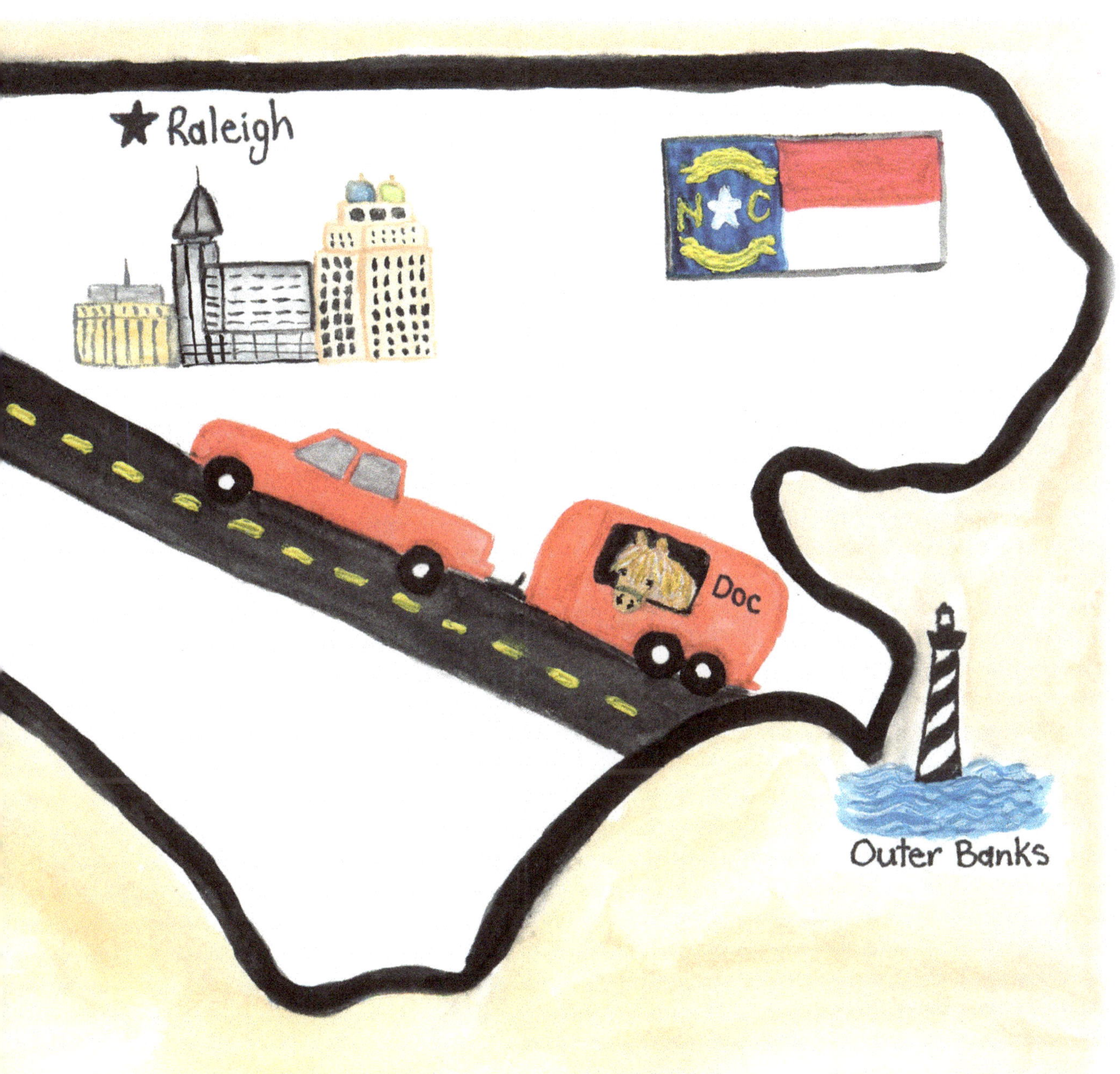

Raleigh
N C
Doc
Outer Banks

When I got out of the trailer, I saw
mountains! They were beautiful and the
air smelled so clean and fresh.
Maybe I would be able to breathe better.

But I did not see any apples.

Miss Ann takes care of all the animals at Southern Sun Farm Sanctuary.

She gives us our breakfast in the morning and hay to eat.

And she always has apples!

If we are good, she also gives us horse cookies and peppermints and more apples.

But she also gives us huge hugs.

I think I like hugs, too!

Just as much as I like apples!

There are also volunteers who clean
up our stalls and give us water to drink.
I like to hang around and watch them.

They bring me apples.
How do they know I like apples?

And
although I
am a very
big boy, I let
the little
girls braid
my mane
and tail.

I do not
mind.
I like boys
and girls.

I let them sit on my back and stand real still
until they feel safe.
Then I take them for a ride just like I did at
the beach.
What fun we have!

And they bring me apples!

I get to hang out in the yard during the day and sleep in my clean stall at night.

It smells good when I go to bed.

I have already met some new friends.
One friend is a donkey, Molly Mae, and
another is Pango, the little pony.
Pango is new to the Farm, too.
She is very small so I look out for her.

She even likes apples!

BUT . . . . It snows in the mountains!
The snow gets in my eyes.
I never saw snow at the beach.
Miss Ann has coats for all of us
to keep warm and dry.

Mine is red . . . the same color as apples!

I love my new home in the mountains!

I can breathe better.
There are boys and girls that visit.
I have a lot of new friends.

Thank you, Miss Ann, the volunteers and
everyone for making

My Forever Home.

And they have lots of apples!

Yum! Apples!

Discussion Questions

1. Is the weather different at the beach and the mountains?

2. What friends did Doc find at his new home?

3. How did Doc get from the beach to the mountains?

4. Does Doc have a favorite food?

5. What is his favorite color?

6. How many apples did Doc eat?

7. Do horses wear coats?

8. What color is Doc's mane?

9. Have you ever moved to a new home?

Thank You To:

My husband, Ken, for his support.

Anna Welsh for her illustrations.

Ann & John Lisk for their dedication to
Southern Sun Farm Sanctuary.

And, of course,
to Doc for his huge personality!

Pam

Look for more adventures of Doc!

Southern Sun Farm Sanctuary

Southern Sun Farm Sanctuary rescues abandoned, abused, neglected and unwanted horses, ponies and donkeys.

It was founded and is directed by Ann and John Lisk. Together, their animal welfare experience spans over 50 years. They are known to take the animals least likely to find a home anywhere else. Some will be adopted into loving forever homes while others will live out their lives at the Sanctuary, their forever home, where they are cared for and cherished.

*"Saving One Horse won't change the World ...
but it will surely change the World for that One Horse."*

To learn more about the Sanctuary or order books, go to: SouthernSunFarm.com / or find us on Facebook

Proceeds from the sale of this book benefit SSFS which is a 501(c)(3) non-profit organization.